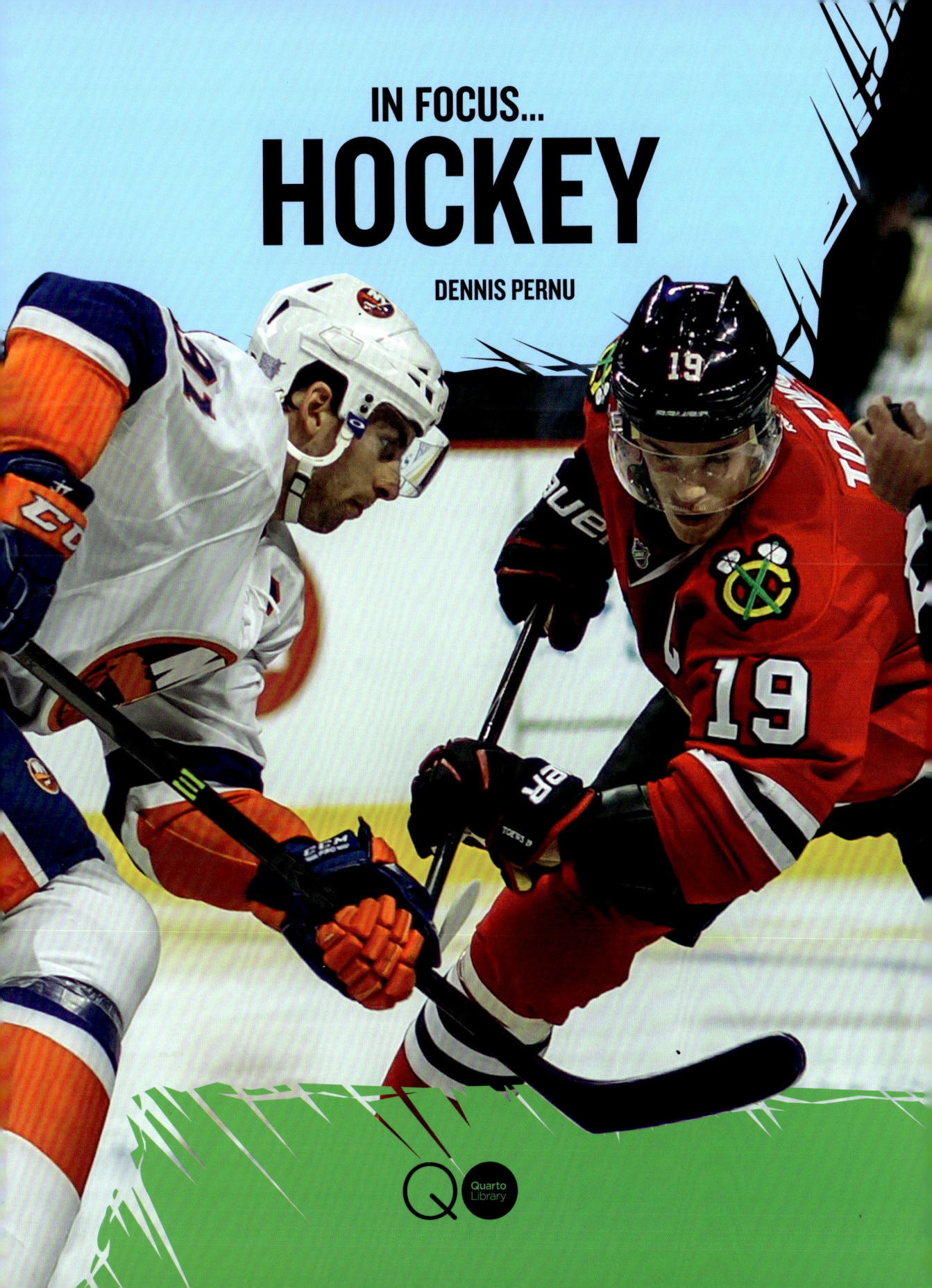

IN FOCUS...
HOCKEY

DENNIS PERNU

Quarto
Library

Quarto is the authority on a wide range of topics.

Quarto educates, entertains and enriches the lives of our readers—enthusiasts and lovers of hands-on living.

www.quartoknows.com

This library edition published in 2019
by Quarto Library,
an imprint of The Quarto Group.
6 Orchard Road
Suite 100
Lake Forest, CA 92630
T: +1 949 380 7510
F: +1 949 380 7575
www.QuartoKnows.com

Distributed in the United States and Canada by
Lerner Publisher Services
241 First Avenue North
Minneapolis, MN 55401 U.S.A.
www.lernerbooks.com

A CIP record for this book is available from the Library of Congress.

ISBN 978 0 7112 4798 7

Manufactured in Guangdong, China CC072019

9 8 7 6 5 4 3 2 1

FSC
www.fsc.org

MIX
Paper from
responsible sources
FSC® C008047

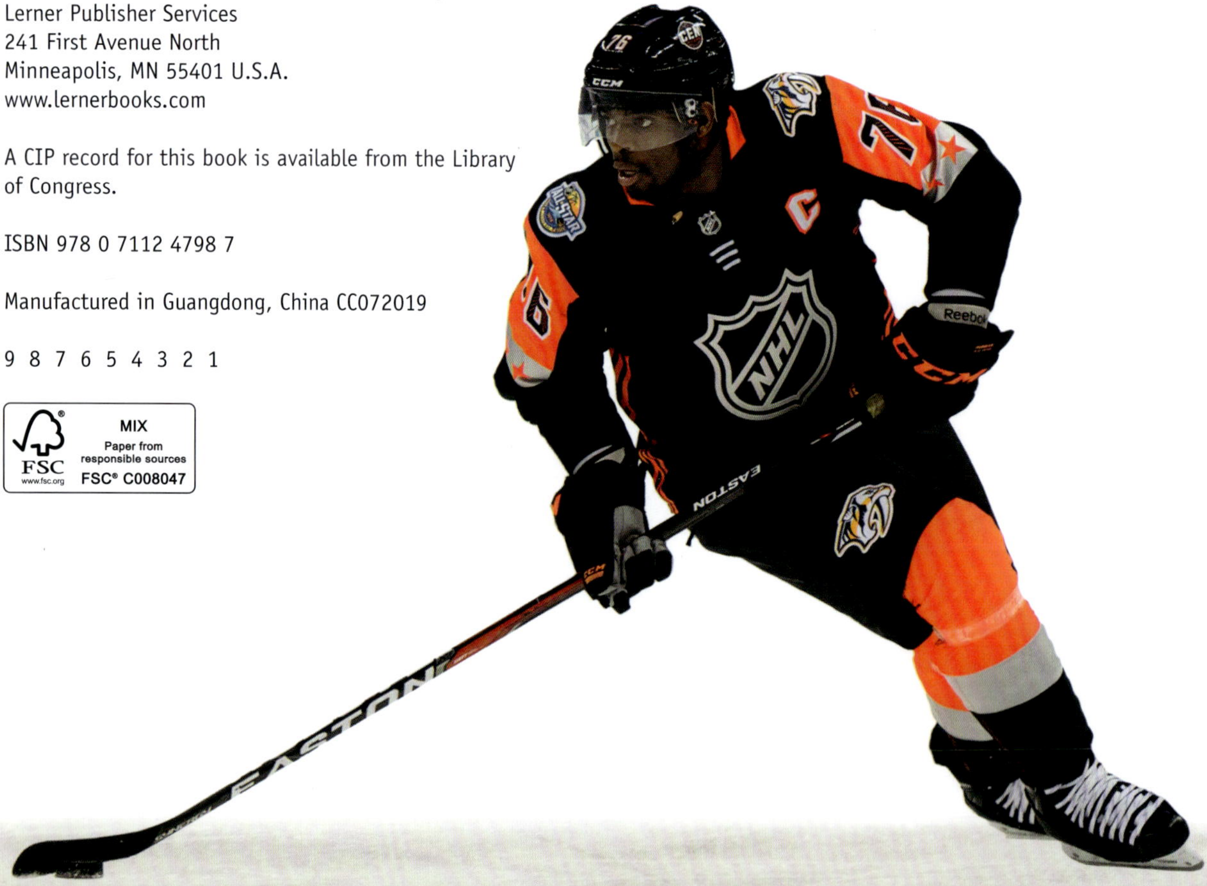

CONTENTS

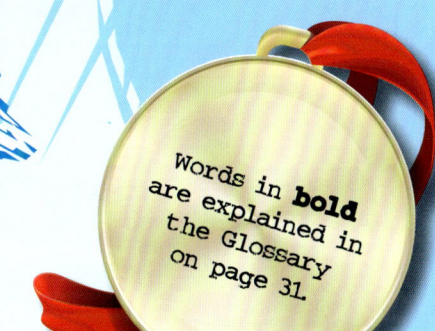

Words in **bold** are explained in the Glossary on page 31.

HOCKEY HISTORY

Hockey's history is rooted in sports from other cultures. Some of these sports were brought to the USA and Canada from Europe. In North America they were combined with games played by Native Americans. As with baseball and football, new rules developed. This led to hockey as we now know it.

Shinty or Shinney?

Two sports from which hockey grew came from very different cultures but share similar names. Shinty is a game played on grass in Scotland. It's been around for more than 2,000 years. Players use curved sticks to shoot a ball into the other team's net. Shinney was a similar stick-and-ball game played by some Native American tribes on huge fields. Today, informal ice hockey played outdoors is known as shinny (with no "e").

Hockey grew from other sports, such as the Scottish game of shinty.

Hockey Is Born

Other sports that were brought to North America included shinty-like games played on skates on rivers in England and the Netherlands. The first indoor game that resembled hockey as we now know it was played in Montreal, Quebec, Canada, on March 3, 1875. By 1900 there were hundreds of teams across Canada. Hockey has long been known as Canada's sport, much as baseball is America's pastime.

Men play ice hockey in Chamonix in the French Alps about 1920.

Many cultures around the world have enjoyed hockey-like sports. This 19th-century engraving shows indigenous people in Chile playing a game called cineca.

WOW!
Hockey players can move fast on their skates—about 30 miles (48 kilometers) per hour!

FACEOFF

LEFT WING

Hockey's ice is called a rink. The rink is surrounded by a wall, or "boards," to keep the puck in play. Most rinks are inside arenas. But hockey is especially popular in areas that have cold winters. There, players enjoy extra ice time on outdoor rinks.

GOALIE

FACEOFF CIRCLE

NET

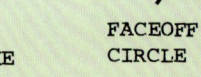

DEFENSEMEN

The Parts of a Rink

In the USA and Canada, most rinks from the youth level to the National Hockey League (NHL) are 200 feet (61 meters) long and 85 feet (26 meters) wide. The middle of the rink, between two blue lines, is the neutral zone. The area from a blue line to the end of the rink is the offensive zone. The rink also has nine faceoff circles. Here, a referee drops the puck between two players to start the action.

A hockey net is made of red steel pipes and nylon mesh. Its opening is 6 feet (1.8 meters) wide and 4 feet (1.2 meters) tall.

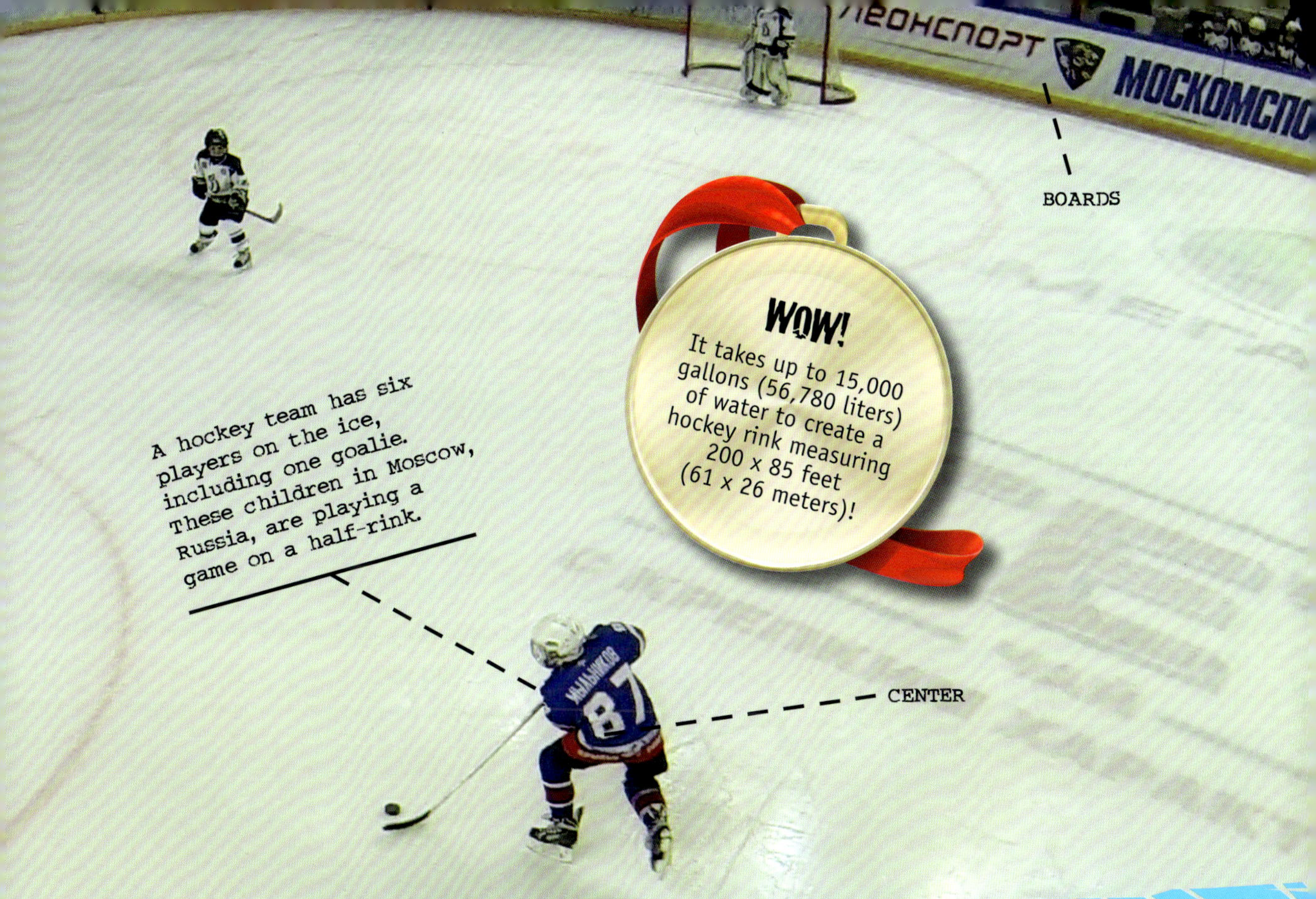
BOARDS
CENTER

A hockey team has six players on the ice, including one goalie. These children in Moscow, Russia, are playing a game on a half-rink.

WOW!
It takes up to 15,000 gallons (56,780 liters) of water to create a hockey rink measuring 200 x 85 feet (61 x 26 meters)!

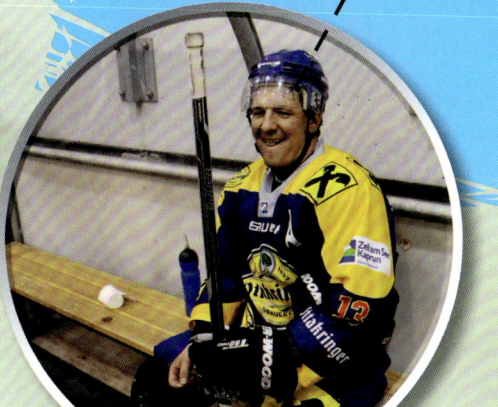

Pass and Shoot

Hockey games are split into three periods. Each team has six players on the ice. They move the puck by passing it to each other. They try to score goals by shooting the puck past their opponents' goalie and into the net. But the other team might suddenly regain control of the puck. The team that was trying to score must quickly switch to playing defense and prevent their opponent from scoring.

When a hockey player breaks a rule, he or she must sit in the penalty box for two or even five minutes. This means their team is a player short.

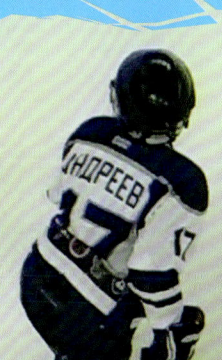

HOCKEY EQUIPMENT

Hockey is a sport with a lot of contact. The players carry sticks and shoot a hard puck. Older players are allowed to **check** each other to get control of the puck. Players must wear special equipment.

HELMET

MASK

SHOULDER PADS

GLOVES

STICK

Hockey is fast and has lots of contact. Players wear gear that protects them.

PUCK

WOW!

Some NHL players go through more than 100 sticks in a single season. Teams spend several hundred thousand dollars on sticks each year.

Skates, Stick, and Puck

For a friendly game of hockey you need three things besides ice: skates, a hockey stick, and a puck. Skates have a leather boot and a sharp steel blade. The blade cuts into the ice so that the player does not slip around. The long L-shaped stick has a blade, too, but it is not sharp. It is used to **stickhandle**, pass, and shoot the puck. Finally, the puck is made of hard rubber and weighs six ounces (170 grams).

A player laces up her skates before a game. Skates are kept sharp with a round, spinning stone that grinds a new edge onto the metal blades.

ELBOW PADS

JERSEY

BREEZERS

SKATES

SHIN PADS

SOCKS

Staying Safe

In games and practices, players wear protective gear. Shin, shoulder, and elbow pads, as well as gloves, are made of dense foam and plastic. Breezers cover the thighs, hips, kidneys, and tailbone. Finally, players at all levels must wear a rugged helmet. Wire masks on younger players' helmets protect their faces from pucks and sticks.

The helmet is an important piece of hockey gear. Kids must also wear a wire mask like this one. Helmets didn't become the rule in the NHL until 1979.

THE GOALIE

There are five positions on a hockey team. The skater positions are center, left and right wing, and two defensive players. The fifth position is goalie. He or she must stop the puck when opponents try to score.

CHEST AND ARM PROTECTORS UNDER JERSEY

MASK

Carey Price is one of the top goalies in the NHL. Check out his equipment!

BLOCKER

Lots of Protection

Goalies wear more protection than their teammates. Hockey pucks are rock hard and travel at high speed. A mask shields the head and face. Chest, arm, and leg pads cover the body. The skates have thick plastic toe caps. Finally, a goalie wears special gloves—a blocker on the hand that holds the stick and a trapper on the other hand to catch pucks. When the goalie stops the puck, it's called a **save**. A goalie who allows no goals in game earns a shutout.

STICK

In 1960 Jacques Plante became the first NHL goalie to regularly wear a mask. He went on to design masks for other goalies, too.

WOW!

In 1928–1929, goalie George Hainsworth won 22 games—all of them by shutout!

Legend of the Crease

The blue area in front of a hockey net is called the crease. Skaters are not allowed in this area. Georges Vezina was one of the early greats to patrol the crease. He played 16 seasons for the Montreal Canadiens (1910–1926). The trophy given to NHL's best goalie is named after him.

Goalies are famous for their superstitions. Patrick Roy once claimed that he talked to his net's metal posts during games.

TRAPPER MITT

LEG PADS

GOALIE SKATES

STAR PROFILE
MARTIN BRODEUR

Born: May 6, 1972 Montreal, Quebec, Canada

Teams: New Jersey Devils, St. Louis Blues

Star Stats: 1,471 games played (1,260 regular season and 205 playoffs), 804 wins, 149 shutouts

THE CENTER

In hockey, a center is the leader of his or her line, which also includes two wings. Most teams have four lines. All of a line's players are allowed to "change on the fly"—leave the ice in the middle of play. A fresh player leaps over the boards to replace them.

Two of the NHL's best centers, Jonathan Toews (#19) and John Tavares (#91), take the faceoff.

Superstar Sidney Crosby leaps over the boards to change on the fly and relieve a tired teammate.

Strong Skaters

A center covers the middle of the ice for the whole length of the rink. In the offensive zone, the center looks for wings to pass the puck to and helps them battle for loose pucks. If his or her team loses the puck, the center must quickly **back check** and help on defense. The center is always in motion. It's no surprise centers are usually a hockey team's best skaters.

12

Superstar Centers

Two of the NHL's best players were centers. Mario Lemieux played 17 seasons (1984–1997, 2000–2006). He racked up 766 goals and 1,129 **assists**. Another center, Wayne Gretzky, is considered by many to be the finest hockey player ever. Known as "The Great One," he holds 60 NHL records. One of today's biggest NHL stars is Sidney Crosby, a center for the Pittsburgh Penguins.

Wayne Gretzky played 21 NHL seasons. He's still the only player to record 200 points in one season—and he did it four times!

STAR PROFILE
WAYNE GRETZKY

Born: January 26, 1961 Brantford, Ontario, Canada

Teams: Edmonton Oilers, Los Angeles Kings, St. Louis Blues, New York Rangers

Star Stats: 1,016 career goals, 2,345 career assists (both NHL records) . . . plus 58 other NHL records!

WOW!
Joe Malone of the old Quebec Bulldogs holds the record for scoring the most goals in one game. He scored seven on January 31, 1920.

WINGS

Wings are the center's linemates. One wing plays on each side of the center: a left wing and right wing. Together, these three are the players most responsible for creating scoring chances.

WOW!

On February 9, 1942, Bill Mosienko of the Chicago Black Hawks scored three goals in just 21 seconds—the quickest **hat trick** in NHL history.

Left wing Alexander Ovechkin Russia (in white) battles a US opponent for the puck during the 2014 World Championships.

Winger Patrick Kane of the Chicago Blackhawks often represents Team USA in international competition.

Puck Control

When the puck goes into the opponents' zone, a wing tries to get to it before an opponent. The other wing might go to the **slot** in front of the net and wait for a pass. Wings also check opponents to gain control of the puck. Like the center, wings must get back and help out on defense too.

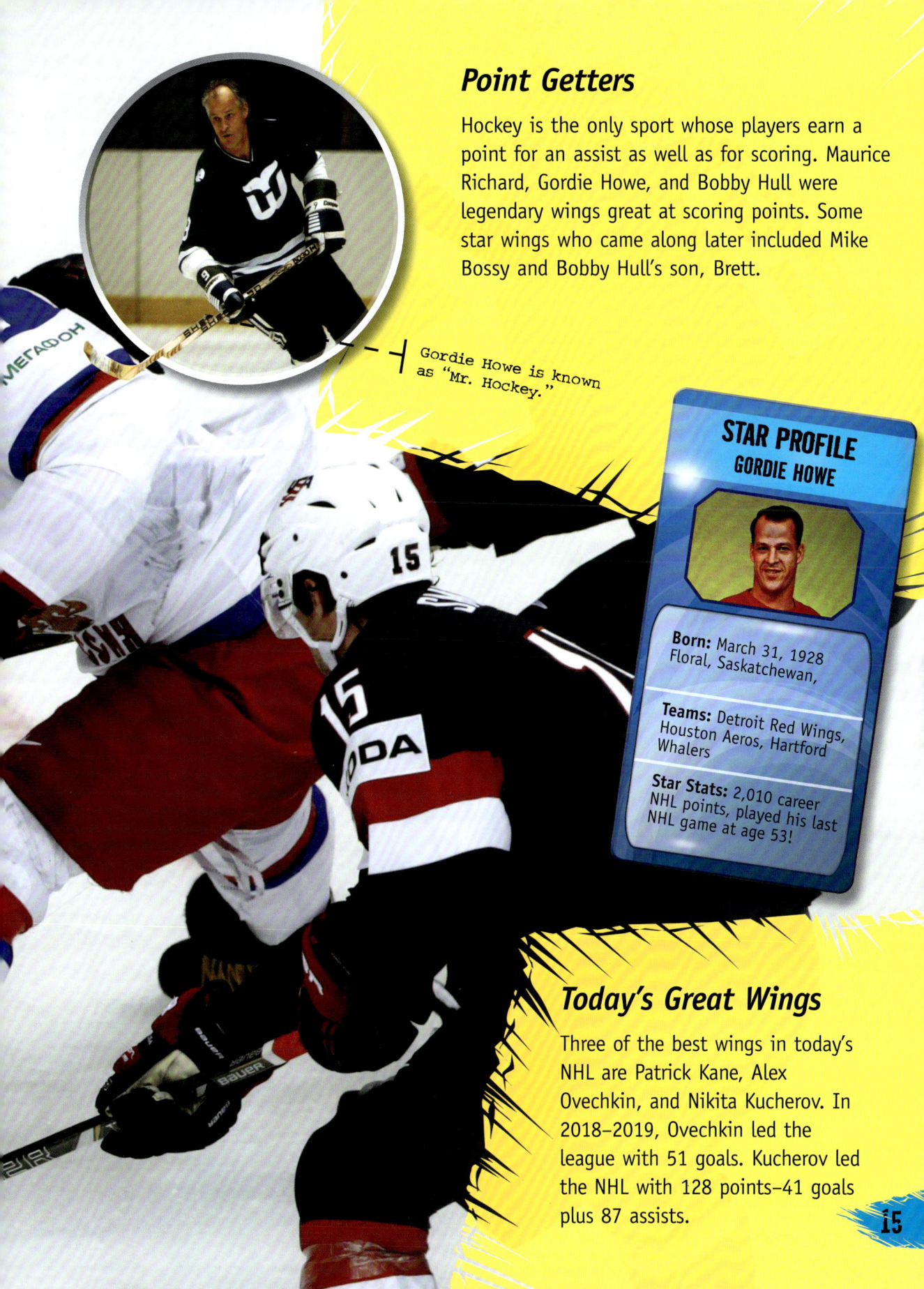

Point Getters

Hockey is the only sport whose players earn a point for an assist as well as for scoring. Maurice Richard, Gordie Howe, and Bobby Hull were legendary wings great at scoring points. Some star wings who came along later included Mike Bossy and Bobby Hull's son, Brett.

Gordie Howe is known as "Mr. Hockey."

STAR PROFILE
GORDIE HOWE

Born: March 31, 1928 Floral, Saskatchewan,

Teams: Detroit Red Wings, Houston Aeros, Hartford Whalers

Star Stats: 2,010 career NHL points, played his last NHL game at age 53!

Today's Great Wings

Three of the best wings in today's NHL are Patrick Kane, Alex Ovechkin, and Nikita Kucherov. In 2018–2019, Ovechkin led the league with 51 goals. Kucherov led the NHL with 128 points–41 goals plus 87 assists.

DEFENSEMEN

Two defensemen are on the ice with the center and wings. Defensemen can score goals and assists, too. Their main job, however, is to prevent the other team's wings and centers from taking shots at their team's net.

WOW!
At 6 feet, 9 inches (2.06 meters), defenseman Zdeno Chara is the tallest player in NHL history.

Big Blueliners

When the puck enters their zone, one defenseman must get to it first. Defensemen move the puck out of their zone with sharp passes to the center or a wing. When the puck is in the offensive zone, defensemen stand just inside the blue line. If the puck comes to them, they keep it in the zone. Sometimes they do this with a **slap shot** at the opposing team's net.

Zdeno Chara of the Boston Bruins holds the record for the fastest slap shot at 108.8 miles (175.1 kilometers) per hour.

Thanks to Orr

Bobby Orr changed the way defensemen play hockey. He entered the NHL in 1966–1967 at 18 years old. Orr showed that defensemen can carry the puck and create scoring chances, too. Thanks to Orr, star defensemen like Washington Capital's John Carlson and Toronto Maple Leaf's Morgan Rielly are scoring threats as well as solid defenders.

Many believe Bobby Orr was the greatest defenseman ever. He proved that a player at his position could be an offensive threat too.

STAR PROFILE
BOBBY ORR

Born: March 20, 1948
Parry Sound, Ontario

Teams: Boston Bruins, Chicago Black Hawks

Star Stats: 102 assists, 139 points in 1970–1971 (single-season NHL records for a defenseman)

Ryan Suter of the Minnesota Wild is a premier NHL defenseman. In 2018–2019 he led the NHL by averaging almost 27 minutes of ice time per game.

THE COACH

A hockey coach is often called the person "behind the bench." This refers to the place where coaches stand during a game. NHL coaches are under a great deal of pressure. If their team doesn't make the playoffs, they might find themselves without a job!

Joel Quenneville seems unhappy with a referee. "Coach Q" leads all current NHL coaches with the most career wins: 890 through the 2018–2019 season.

Toronto Maple Leafs head coach Mike Babcock is considered one of the NHL's best coaches. He has also coached the Anaheim Ducks and Detroit Red Wings.

Brain behind the Bench

Head coaches choose their team's **roster**. They also decide what strategies their team will use throughout the season. They hold practice sessions for their teams almost every day—even before games. During a game, the coach changes his team's lines to give them the best matchup against their opponents. Luckily, coaches usually have several assistant coaches to help them.

STAR PROFILE
SCOTTY BOWMAN

Born: September 18, 1933 Peterborough, Ontario

Teams: St. Louis Blues, Montreal Canadiens, Buffalo Sabres, Pittsburgh Penguins, Detroit Red Wings

Star Stats: 1,481 career coaching wins, 9x Stanley Cup champion (both NHL records)

In one 1928 game, New York Rangers' coach Lester Patrick stepped in to play for his injured goalie—and led his team to victory!

From Toe to Joel

One of the greatest NHL coaches ever was Toe Blake. He led the Montreal Canadiens to eight Stanley Cups in 13 seasons (1955–1968). Scotty Bowman, a former paint salesman, also coached the Canadiens. He still holds the record for most coaching wins and Stanley Cups championships. Joel Quenneville is the current NHL coach with the most wins.

19

WOMEN'S HOCKEY

Women's hockey teams have been around since the 1800s. In the last 20 years, however, women's and girls' hockey has become popular at the youth, college, and professional levels. Today, more than 100 US colleges and universities have women's hockey teams. In Canada there are more than 30 university teams.

WOW!
The University of Minnesota women's team won 62 straight games from February 2012 to November 2013. That's a record for both men's and women's hockey.

The Basics

The rules of women's hockey are mostly the same as those for the men's game. The major difference is that body checking is not allowed in women's hockey. Like boys, girls can begin playing hockey at an early age. At the youngest levels it is common for boys and girls to learn the basic skills together.

Loren Gabel (#19) of Clarkson University was named the best player in women's college hockey for the 2018–2019 season.

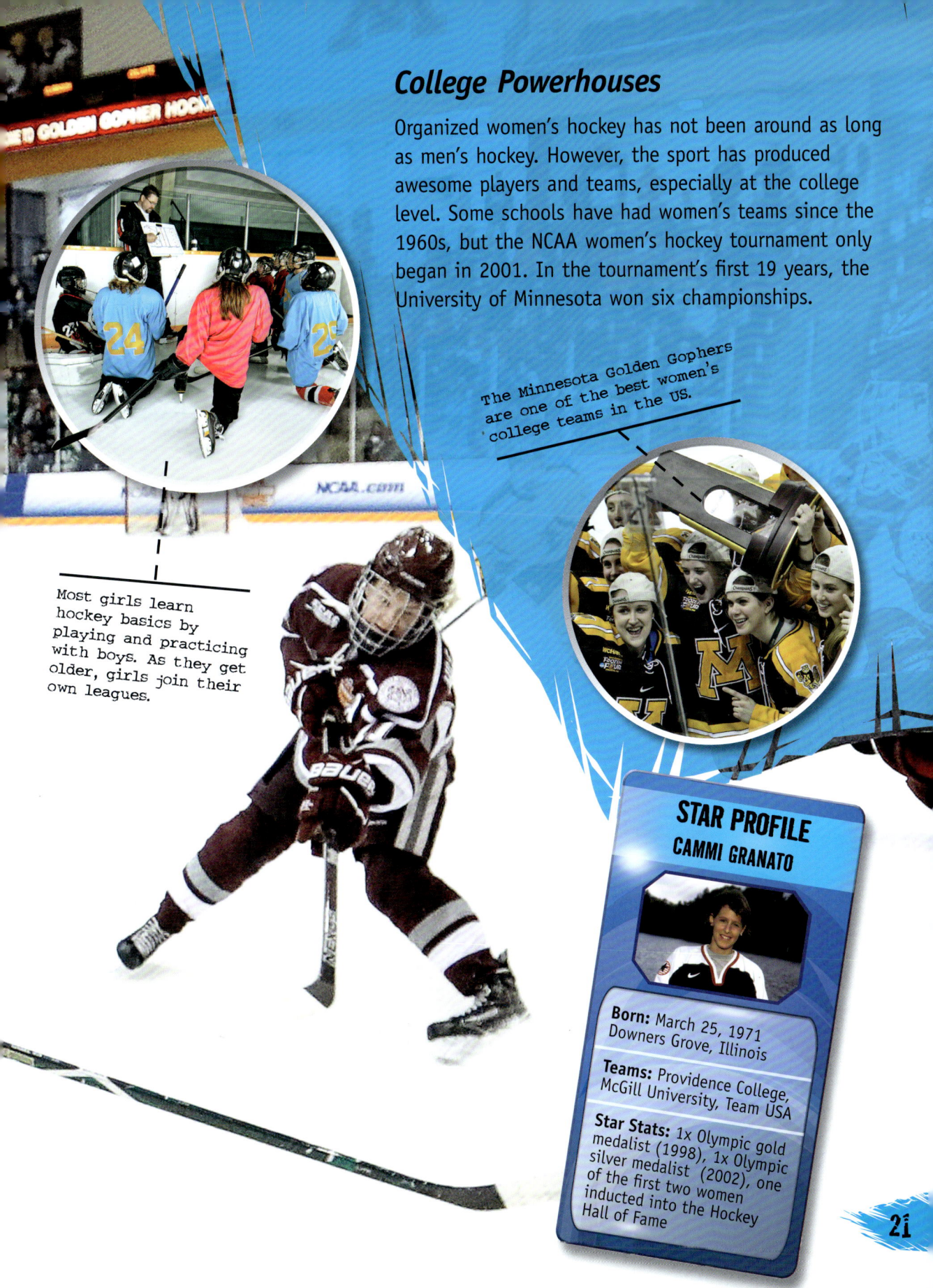

College Powerhouses

Organized women's hockey has not been around as long as men's hockey. However, the sport has produced awesome players and teams, especially at the college level. Some schools have had women's teams since the 1960s, but the NCAA women's hockey tournament only began in 2001. In the tournament's first 19 years, the University of Minnesota won six championships.

The Minnesota Golden Gophers are one of the best women's college teams in the US.

Most girls learn hockey basics by playing and practicing with boys. As they get older, girls join their own leagues.

STAR PROFILE
CAMMI GRANATO

Born: March 25, 1971 Downers Grove, Illinois

Teams: Providence College, McGill University, Team USA

Star Stats: 1x Olympic gold medalist (1998), 1x Olympic silver medalist (2002), one of the first two women inducted into the Hockey Hall of Fame

INTERNATIONAL HOCKEY

Hockey has been popular in Canada and the northern USA for more than a century. But it's a very popular sport in other nations, too. Today, more than 25 percent of NHL players are from Europe. And more and more European players are joining college teams in the USA and junior teams in Canada.

WOW!

Russia (formerly the Soviet Union) has won 27 World Championships gold medals versus Canada's 26. From 1963 to 1990, the Soviets won 20 of 25 world titles.

Some NHL players get the chance to play for their countries at international tournaments. Here Finland battles their rival Sweden.

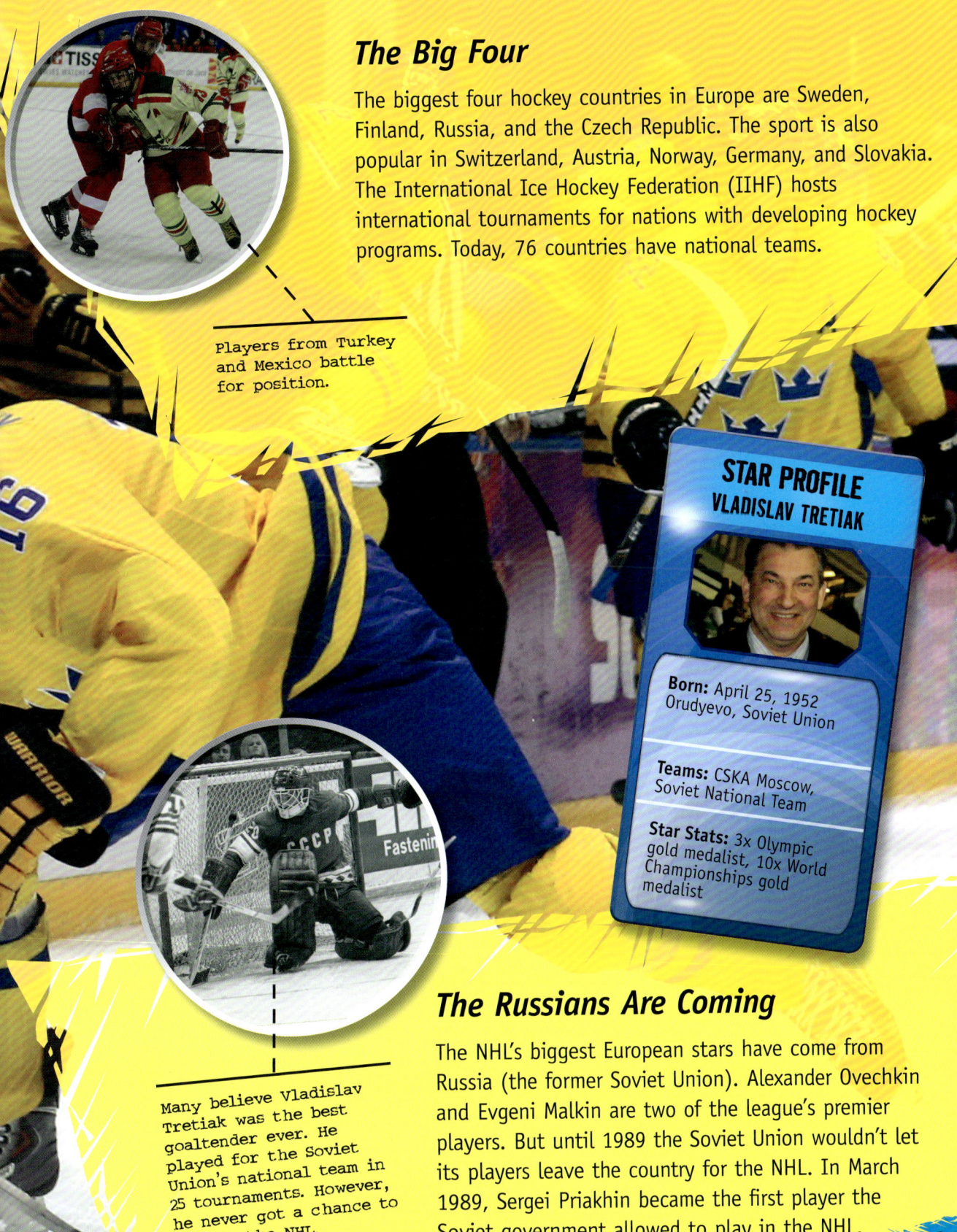

The Big Four

The biggest four hockey countries in Europe are Sweden, Finland, Russia, and the Czech Republic. The sport is also popular in Switzerland, Austria, Norway, Germany, and Slovakia. The International Ice Hockey Federation (IIHF) hosts international tournaments for nations with developing hockey programs. Today, 76 countries have national teams.

Players from Turkey and Mexico battle for position.

STAR PROFILE
VLADISLAV TRETIAK

Born: April 25, 1952 Orudyevo, Soviet Union

Teams: CSKA Moscow, Soviet National Team

Star Stats: 3x Olympic gold medalist, 10x World Championships gold medalist

Many believe Vladislav Tretiak was the best goaltender ever. He played for the Soviet Union's national team in 25 tournaments. However, he never got a chance to play in the NHL.

The Russians Are Coming

The NHL's biggest European stars have come from Russia (the former Soviet Union). Alexander Ovechkin and Evgeni Malkin are two of the league's premier players. But until 1989 the Soviet Union wouldn't let its players leave the country for the NHL. In March 1989, Sergei Priakhin became the first player the Soviet government allowed to play in the NHL, when he joined the Calgary Flames.

23

THE STANLEY CUP

Hockey's greatest prize is the Stanley Cup. It's the oldest pro sports trophy in North America. Each year, 31 NHL teams begin the season hoping they'll be the ones to lift the Cup at season's end. But only one team can win—that's what makes the Stanley Cup so special.

WOW!
As of 2014, the Stanley Cup had 3,073 names engraved on it—and 14 of those had been misspelled!

Lord of the Rings

The Stanley Cup is named for Lord Stanley of Preston, the former governor of Canada. He had the trophy made to give to Canada's top **amateur** hockey club each year. In 1915 Canada's pro teams took over the Cup. The Stanley Cup is much taller now than when it was first made. That is because rings have been added at the bottom, engraved with the names of players on the winning teams.

The bowl at the top is a replica of the original donated by Lord Stanley in 1892.

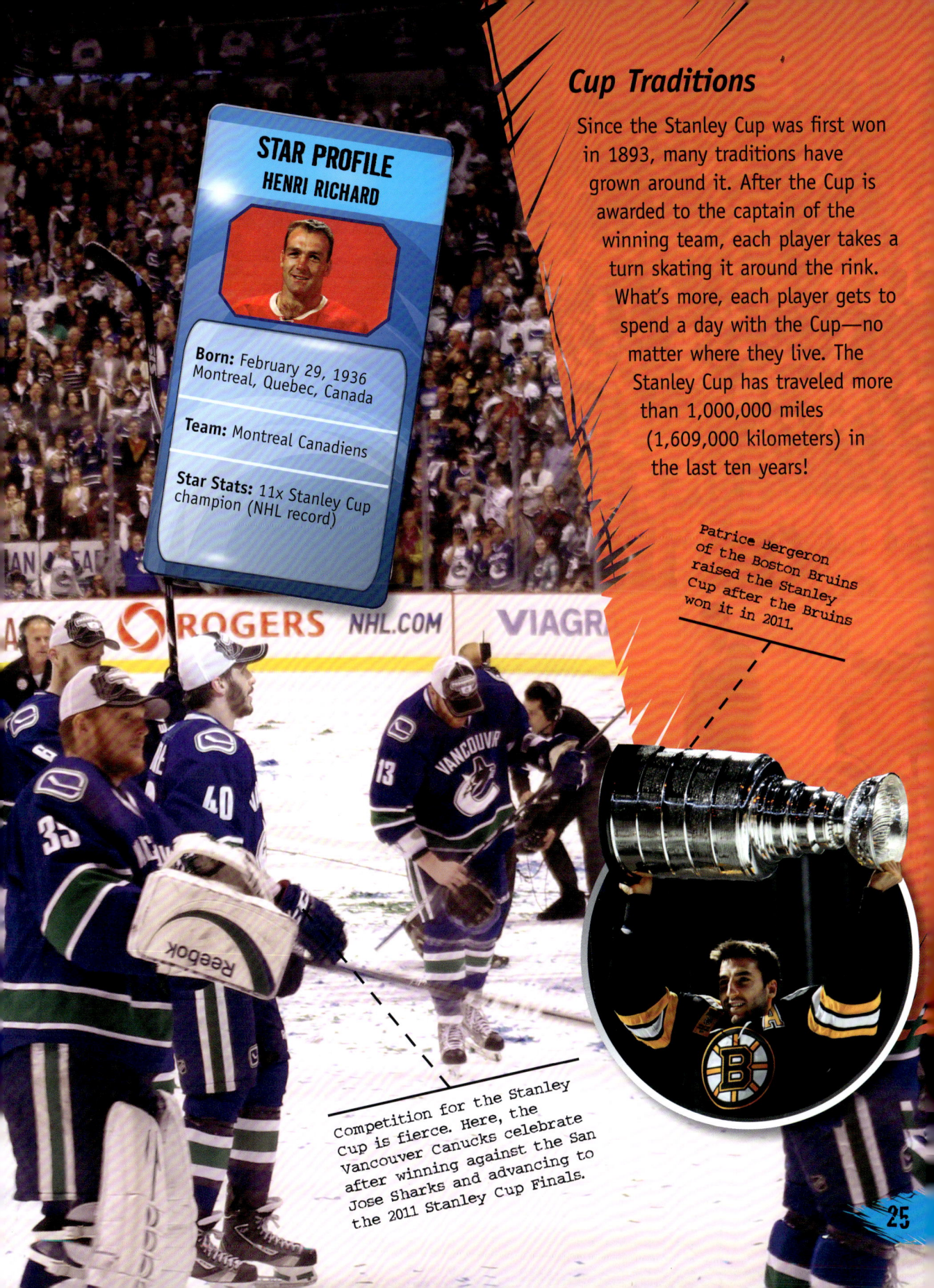

STAR PROFILE
HENRI RICHARD

Born: February 29, 1936
Montreal, Quebec, Canada

Team: Montreal Canadiens

Star Stats: 11x Stanley Cup champion (NHL record)

Cup Traditions

Since the Stanley Cup was first won in 1893, many traditions have grown around it. After the Cup is awarded to the captain of the winning team, each player takes a turn skating it around the rink. What's more, each player gets to spend a day with the Cup—no matter where they live. The Stanley Cup has traveled more than 1,000,000 miles (1,609,000 kilometers) in the last ten years!

Patrice Bergeron of the Boston Bruins raised the Stanley Cup after the Bruins won it in 2011.

Competition for the Stanley Cup is fierce. Here, the Vancouver Canucks celebrate after winning against the San Jose Sharks and advancing to the 2011 Stanley Cup Finals.

ALL-STAR GAME

January is the halfway point of the NHL season. For one week, most NHL players get a break from the long schedule. Other players are chosen to take part in the All-Star Game. Fans vote for their favorite players to compete against each other in this special **exhibition game**.

In 2019 USA Olympic player Kendall Coyne Schofield became the first woman to take part in the NHL All Star Skills Competition.

Edmonton Oiler Connor McDavid is the NHL's fastest skater.

Best of the Best

The NHL All-Star Game is held in a different city each year. The first one was played in 1947 in Toronto, Canada. Until 1969, one all-star team made up of the league's best players faced the Stanley Cup champions. Today, there is one all-star team for each of the league's four divisions. Every NHL team has at least one player in the All-Star Game. Fans can see popular players from throughout the league compete in one event.

Nashville Predators defenseman P. K. Subban skates up the ice during the 2018 NHL All Star Game.

STAR PROFILE
GLENN HALL

Born: October 3, 1931 Humboldt, Saskatchewan, Canada

Teams: Detroit Red Wings, Chicago Black Hawks, St. Louis Blues

Star Stats: 13 All-Star Game appearances (NHL record for goalies)

Three Against Three

Today's All-Star Game is really a four-team tournament. The winners of the two **semifinal** games battle to decide the overall winners. Instead of five skaters, each team has just three skaters and one goalie on the ice. Fewer defensive skaters result in more goals—and very entertaining games. Before the games, players have a Skills Competition to decide which all-star is the fastest skater and most accurate shooter.

DROP THE PUCK!

Hockey is a fantastic sport famous for its speed and intense competition. But the best thing about the sport is that it's fun. You don't have to be a pro to get in on it. Sometimes you don't even need ice!

Hockey is very popular in many cold-weather areas. These two boys are taking a break from a game of shinny on their backyard rink.

Rink Rats

Hockey can be addictive. People who hang out at ice rinks all day are called "rink rats." During the winter, some even build backyard rinks so they can skate whenever they want. In colder areas, public parks have outdoor rinks with skates and sticks you can borrow. And some NHL teams host "Learn to Play Hockey" days. You can try on gear, get on the ice, and find out if hockey's for you.

Sled hockey is played by athletes who are unable to walk. Players use two short sticks to move themselves around the ice and to shoot the puck.

All Kinds of Hockey

Fans and players of all ages enjoy hockey. Some players learn to skate as soon as they can walk. And people who cannot walk can take part in the game on sleds. Hockey is enjoyed without ice, too. Street hockey is played on a driveway or outdoor basketball court. Floor hockey is popular in gym classes. There's even roller hockey, which is played on inline skates. Whichever you choose, you'll find that this great sport can be for everyone.

A small ball like a tennis ball and sticks with tough plastic blades are all that are needed for a game of street hockey. You can even play on inline skates.

WOW! High school hockey is very popular in some states. In 2019, 106,895 fans attended the Minnesota State High School Hockey Tournament.

CREDITS

AUTHOR'S NOTE

I hope you have enjoyed reading all about the history, rules, and superstars of hockey! Maybe you and your friends were even inspired to get outside and give hockey a try.

Over the years I have had the pleasure of writing books about many different topics, from hot rod cars to haunted houses, but sports have always been one of my favorite things to write (and read!) about. When I was a youngster in school, most of my reading time was spent learning about sports stars of years past. I was also lucky to participate in several sports, often at the encouragement of my parents, including ice hockey, baseball, tennis, football, golf, and even BMX racing. I was never the best among my peers in any of those sports, but it turns out that wasn't the point. I learned all about teamwork from some of my great coaches (like Lowell Thomas and Randy Reigstad), made lifelong friends, collected favorite memories, and got plenty of exercise!

Today I live in Minneapolis, Minnesota. It is known as the "City of Lakes" and it is a wonderful place to get outside and be active throughout the year. There's fishing, canoeing, bicycling, and swimming in the summer, and skating, sledding, and skiing during the long winters. The parks offer sports leagues for kids of all ages, and today I am lucky to pay forward the lessons I learned from those fantastic coaches of my youth by coaching my sons, Leo and Gus, and their ice hockey teams.

Keep reading, but keep moving, too!

Dennis Pernu

GLOSSARY

amateur
an athlete who is not paid to play their sport; the opposite of professional

assist
a point that's awarded to a player who passes the puck to a teammate who then scores; assists are not recorded on the scoreboard

back check
to quickly skate back to the defensive zone and help prevent the opponent from scoring

check
to knock an opponent away from the puck by hitting them with a shoulder or hip

exhibition game
a game played purely for fun or entertainment

hat trick
a feat in hockey or soccer in which one player scores three goals in a single game

roster
a list of the members of a sports team

save
when a goaltender stops the puck from crossing the goal line

semifinal
a game that determines one of the two teams that will advance to the championship game

slap shot
hitting a puck sharply with the stick to send it toward the opponent's net at great speed

slot
the area right in front of the hockey goal crease

stats
numbers used in any sport to measure an athlete's performance

stickhandle
to control a puck by dribbling it back and forth with the blade of a hockey stick

INDEX